The Year of the Bird

true stories in pictures & words

A GRAPHIC JOURNAL

written and illustrated

by Susan Spangler

THE YEAR OF THE BIRD
(true stories in pictures & words)
written and illustrated by Susan Spangler

Published by Little Known Stories
22 Virginia Drive
Gaithersburg, MD 20877
www.littleknownstories.com

© Copyright 2011 by Susan Spangler

ISBN 978-0-9840316-3-4

All rights reserved. No part of this publication may be reproduced, stored in a retrieval system, or transmitted in any form or by any means - electronic, mechanical, photocopy, recording, or any other - except for brief quotations in printed reviews, without the prior written permission of the author.

Cover and text design by Susan Spangler

contents

1   finding words

the bird

7   year of the bird

the kids

21   day after new year's
25   saying words
27   tonight's blessing
29   birthday party at the soccerplex
31   storytellers
35   negotiation
37   kindergarten girl
40   melanie's questions
43   jeremy thinks about the future
45   the shoe man's story
49   not full yet

jean

53   keepsakes
55   this week at the doctors' with jean
61   stuart and francine
65   tornado warning
71   wednesday afternoon with jean in her hospice room

home

75 signs of spring
77 edible flowers
79 passover stories
85 watering the plants
87 sniper
89 life in the asteroid belt
91 time out for romance
95 a month before war
97 praise for our rubbermaid mailbox

letting go

103 reunion
110 letting go 101
115 violets
119 one day the bird flies away
122 thanks

finding words

finding words

At a loss for words again today

I take myself away to Brookside Gardens.

I gaze up tall trees seeking peace

and deep into thickets, longing for light.

I study stillness in rocks

and crouch close to red berries, seeking joy.

Yellow lilies bigger than hands bloom in bunches.

A turtle the size of a bowl skims the surface of a pond.

Leafy shadows sway on
gray stepping stones.

Pathways curve between trees. I keep reminding myself—look up, look up.

You, thoughts of you, are with me
every step, every breath.

Clouds overhead   bird on the wind   blossoms   stones   water   sky

I've gone away today
in search of words.

   Words
   to help me
   understand.

   Words
   to share
   with you.

With all my love, these are the words

I've found for you
today.

the bird

DECEMBER 2001

year of the bird

This is the year I discovered my husband, George, loves a bird.

All this time together—pets, daughters, sons-in-law, grandchildren—I thought I had his number: no more surprises. Hah! My mistake, as I should have realized when this same man who used to muse about becoming a vegan decided that a diet of meat and cheese was just the thing for him.

Well, somehow all I managed to learn from that was that he really does love meat. And cheese.

This bird came out of nowhere.

Actually, not nowhere.

Actually, the playground, sitting on a branch. Clearly not a creature native to the temperate zone, but a lost pet, flown the coop. Our daughter, Jenny, is pushing her kids on the swings when the bird catches her eye. She clucks to it, holds out her finger, the bird hops aboard, and, just like she's done since she was a kid, she brings it home—the latest in a long line of rescued critters, protected in boxes or the back yard until their owners show up to claim them.

Jenny's friend, Gary, a man who loves birds, brings over a cage and bird food and a book about cockatiels, which this one, it turns out, is.

All this happens while I'm getting my hair cut. By the time I get home, the kids are taking a vote on what to name the bird, Rocky or Tweety. I don't want to vote. I think, "Oh brother, the last thing I want in this house is a bird." Kevin insists. I vote for Rocky. Rocky wins.

I guess I probably have some surprises in me, too. George certainly looked surprised that night he came home and found I'd painted giant butterflies all over the dining room wall.

Now back to the bird.

My feeling about birds:
I like them. Outside.

I love hearing their peeping and chirping in the yard and watching ducks ripple and dive in a pond.

I love to catch the sight of a black vee of honking geese flapping across a patch of pink and gray sky.

For a couple of springs, a nest of baby cardinals hatched right next to the screen porch. We took pictures.

But inside, in a cage, it's just different for me. Maybe partly the cage itself, the bars around the jailbird, whose main claim to fame is, after all, its wings.

Dogs and cats, they get to run around the yard. Even a fish in a bowl gets to swim. A bird's gotta fly. But in my living room?

Who am I kidding? It isn't that I'm such a compassionate animal lover. I'm not. I just don't want the noise. I don't want the mess. Don't want a bird in the house. Never have.

But George.

We both love to talk. And over the years we've covered a lot of ground. For instance: I knew he'd entertained thoughts of raising llamas. And on occasion he's mentioned chickens.

So even though it didn't really compute in the moment, when I reconstruct that first afternoon with the bird—our daughter Jenny, our three grandkids, plus our two big dogs roaming in circles around us, their heavy tails thumping against the kitchen chairs—I can remember hearing George's voice saying, "I love this bird!"

As it turns out, no one ever calls back about this bird. And it's still in its cage, right next to the dining room table, on top of the built-in cabinet by the front door, whistling and trilling and peeping like a car alarm, dropping feathers and millet and who-knows-what-else all over the dining room floor.

But here's the important thing: this bird has become more than a bird.

It's become a last straw on that camel's back. It's become a bird of contention. And how surprising is that?

This is 2001, a year thundering with contention, a hell of a year. Actually a year that started three years ago.

Because it was three years ago that John—Jenny's husband, our son-in-law—got sick. Out of the blue, he had the worst kind of brain cancer. He was thirty-three years old then, quiet, gentle, brave, terrified. Their kids were six months, two and four.

George and I hired a contractor right away to finish off enough space to fit us all into our house, and Jenny and John and the kids moved in. John lived here about a year before he died upstairs in their bedroom in Jenny's arms, both of them in my arms, George on the bed with us, too, wiping John's face with a washcloth, John's last words, to Jenny—"I love you"—June 30, 2000.

But stop.

That's just three sentences. Too short. Just a glide down a slide into the pool at the end.

Between the top and the bottom there's brain cancer, which we found out quickly doesn't happen just inside the brain, but also in whatever parts of the body are attached to the parts of the brain where the tumor is frantically putting down roots. In John's case, that was his motor strip—who'd ever heard of that before—which we soon learned was connected to his arms and legs.

Sometimes people have blinding headaches and think, oh my god, I might have a brain tumor. Usually they don't. But sometimes it's actually true.

But that wasn't the way it worked with John. With him, it was so quiet, so modest, you could almost call it discreet: his left pinkie felt numb. Sometimes he couldn't make it hit the "A" key on his computer.

It took a month from that to get to the diagnosis. By then he could hardly move his left arm, and his left leg had started to drag; that's how fast things started changing once the tumor got his attention.

Metaphors happen.

You don't ever have to look far for them: they spring into life out of what you've just seen, what you've heard, smelled, touched. That must be why they feel so satisfying, why they're so unforgettable, so real you almost feel you're gripping them in your fist.

You can't help loving a good metaphor. I've read that in the 1700's the brain was imagined to work like a clock, then by the mid 1800's and on into the 1900's like a machine. And now, of course, we all think that it works like a computer.

This year, 2001, has brought us terrorism. And that's what, if you didn't already know, brain cancer is like.

One minute everything seems fine, and then the next, the cancer plane crashes into the tall tower of John (who really was tall, and thin and shy, his long brown hair in a ponytail halfway down his back, who cooked like a gourmet, who noticed everything and read almost a book a day, who cried at sad movies and drove fast, who watched TV half the night and loved to hold his kids and kiss his wife).

The cancer plane hits the tower of John, whose structure is solidly grounded to absorb all manner of lesser difficulties and keep on standing. But this terrorist takes his arm and then his leg and gives him seizures and takes away his power to stand and then to sit and then to read and to swallow and to talk and then to breathe.

At first the doctors tell us John has eight months to a year, and he makes it to eighteen months, about a year of that in our house, all of us living here together.

We drink our coffee in the morning, do the dishes, take care of the kids, argue, kid, something like normal. John actually cooks dinner for us almost every night as long as he can stand.

If anyone asks, he says, "I'm doing excellent."

The radiation seems to stop it for a while. Acupuncture helps to ease the pain. But the tumor. It takes his life away.

It takes him away from us.

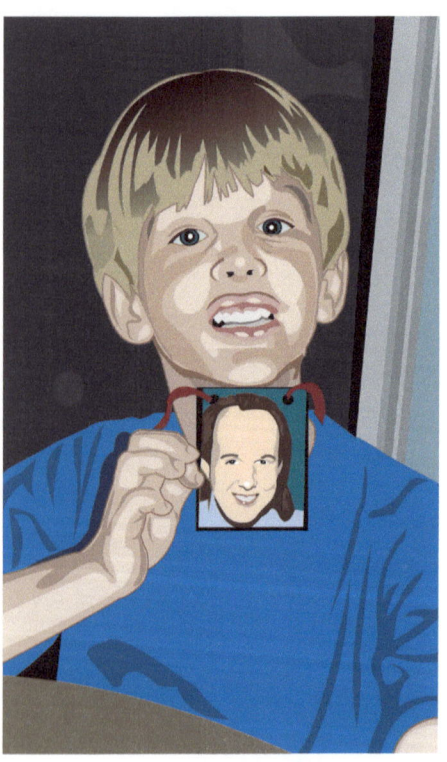

All the kids grieve. But Kevin, age five, the oldest, takes it the hardest. After John dies, Kevin doesn't want to leave the house and spends a lot of time Scotch-taping cans and bottles from the recycling bin into bulging, bulky spaceships that he tells us can fly away into the sky.

All summer and fall the kids cry out, "I want Daddy!" from their beds at night. Stroking their heads, we say, "We want him, too."

It's true. We feel his absence in our swollen silences. Like pieces from different puzzles, we move ourselves around, but can't quite fit.

When first grade starts, Jenny and I both go to meet Kevin's teacher, to introduce her to this precious boy whose special qualities might not be apparent to her. Which they aren't. It's a hard year.

But the summer after is peaceful for him. He makes lots of new things using much less Scotch tape. And in the fall he starts at a new school, which he loves right away.

September 11.

It's Kevin's seventh birthday.

George and I are still in bed, the radio tuned to NPR, when we hear the first confused report. A small plane? An accident? We make coffee and turn on CNN, the terrorism marathon: all terrorism, all the time.

Jenny drives back to the school and picks up the kids as soon as the second tower falls. That afternoon, Kevin builds a three-foot replica of the World Trade Center out of paper and Scotch-tapes it inside a box.

Anthrax gets mailed here to Washington on my birthday. I scan the sky for small planes spraying poison. Each bright blue morning I think: maybe this is the last. I cry when I sing the kids to sleep. I'm scared all the time. George tunes in the speculating heads on TV when we get into bed at night. We argue, both of us angry.

I can't sleep. I remember my Jewish great-grandmothers, how they brought their families to America from Czarist Russia and Poland and Rumania a hundred years ago. How they saved them from danger. I come from them, I think. I can do what they did. I consider Canada or Minnesota, someplace cold and safe.

But then, instead of saving anyone, I start painting murals all over the house. Giant butterflies in the dining room. Pictures of our dogs and cats at the end of the hall. I paint tall trees in fall colors and a purple sky all over the living room arch and four more walls a deep yellow-gold.

Then, around four one morning

George's mother Jean calls us on the phone and says she can't breathe. We call 911.

It's her second heart attack in a year. At the E.R. they ask us if we want them to put her on a ventilator and we say, "Yes! Of course!"

And she starts breathing again, and we take her home after a few days—to the house she bought in 1953—a sturdy house in the shape of a rectangle on a corner lot, the house where George and his younger brother, Robert, and their older sister, Susan, grew up, and where George and Robert lived together in the '70s while Jean was in Vietnam working for the army, until George went off to law school and Robert left for Arizona—the house where Jean lived on her own, almost fifty years in all.

But now Jean is 84 and so weak that just standing up makes her dizzy, and she can't remember her pills or even to eat much more than a half a saltine at a time.

"I'm not myself," she says when we come in, not the quick-witted, sharp-tongued, high-heeled gal who'd kept her house after her divorce and raised her kids and retired from her job at the Pentagon, where she'd worked her way up with nobody's help but her own.

Well, mothers get old, if you're lucky. It's a familiar story. You sell the house and sort through the stuff with her and sell some of it to the neighbors at a yard sale on a rainy Saturday. You move her to an assisted living place and fix up her new room, so it feels like home.

But that's not the whole story here. Robert, who's been living in Jean's basement since he moved back from Arizona years ago, figured they'd live in the house together forever. Never mind that once in a while she yells at him about some little thing and then forgets and yells at him again. Never mind how fed up that makes him feel. Never mind how old she is; she's always taken real good care of herself.

"Mom's gonna outlive us all!" he'd predict.

After the house is sold and emptied out, he sits alone in the dark living room night after night in the only chair left, smoking and watching The Weather Channel. When George and I drive by on the hot July morning when the new owners are scheduled to arrive, Robert's truck is gone.

Now comes the bird.

Okay, I know. We've all heard of birds.
We know what a bird is.

This isn't brain surgery or brain cancer. It's not death or the grief of young wives and small children. It isn't collapsing buildings or poisoned mail or a beloved mother growing old and sick or a childhood home sold to strangers.

It isn't a younger brother who disappeared for six months and told you, after finally showing up at the door the week before Christmas, that he's broke and living in a tent. It doesn't make us feel mystified or terrified or unbearably sad, like some other things we might be thinking about.

Right?

It's perfectly clear. I know just how I feel: I want to give the bird away to someone who wants it, which our friend Pam actually does.

And George?

George loves the bird. He wants to keep it.

In fact, he's going to keep it. Got it?

Help me out. What's the fair thing here? I know husbands and wives all have their secret formulas, continually recalibrating the fine line between playing fair. And not.

Take for example, oh, three years ago, when I gave in on the cat, now it's your turn, give in on the bird.

No.

Or. You promised you'd clean up after the bird, and you haven't, so now let's give the bird away.

Yes, I have.

Then what's that right there on the floor?

Give me a break.

You said if I still didn't want the bird in two months we could give it away. It's been three. I still don't.

I love the bird.

Okay, let's try a different tack. How about this:

Keep the bird.

What can I say? You want it, I don't. Who can parse what's fair in there?

It's just a bird, after all. Let's just say this is the year of the bird. Twigs, seeds, dust, scraps of treasures, hatchlings circling with open mouths, chatter, clutter, unexpected screeches, flashes of color, whooshes of wings.

This is the year I discovered my husband and I both have plenty of surprises left in us, and that, next to what the rest of life can dish up, our surprises are, if not exactly chopped liver, then at least reasonably small potatoes.

So bearing in mind, of course, that there can never, ever be a year of the llama or the chicken or, God forbid, the snake, let's just sit back a minute and watch another ball go down, have another good night kiss, hold on tight, and go on from here into next year.

the kids

JANUARY 2002

day after new year's

Today, bright and cold again, it's just the kids and me.

I drink three cups of coffee before we pick up Jeremy from nursery school. We stop at the grocery store on the way home: don't touch, sit down, stand here, everyone hold hands.

At home, the littler ones watch a movie in the bedroom while Kevin, age seven, and I take down the ornaments and the lights and drag the Christmas tree and the dining room rug out the front door, sweeping and sweeping pine needles as we go. We lay the rug on the garden wall, and Kevin happily whacks off more pine needles with the broom.

By the time we carry the rug back into the house, he's almost out of gas, but he stays with it and helps me lift the dining room table back into its position in the center of the room. Two stars for such good helping.

Then everyone puts on coats and gets zipped up, and Jeremy and I grab the trunk end and Melanie and Kevin each hold a skinny branch near the pointy top, and together we carry the bare tree out the driveway, around the corner and down the street to the woods.

Halfway down, we change positions, so everyone can have a chance to lead the way, and when we get there we all agree it's a good idea to prop our tree up against an old tall trunk.

Our hands sticky with sap, our shoes submerged under the blanketing layers of brown leaves, we stand before our tree, small here in the woods, holding hands. "Would you like to say some words?" I ask.

Kevin says, "I love you, Christmas tree! Thank you! Good-bye!"

Melanie says, "Thank you, Christmas tree, for visiting our house and staying with us for a while! We love you! Good-bye! We'll come see you in the summer!"

"In our bathing suits!" Jeremy says.

Back inside, the house is clean and straight, the rose-colored rug soft, yellow walls glowing. I make supper, the kids and I sit down to eat.

Jenny comes home from her holiday trip with presents and shiny cardboard souvenirs from New Year's Eve: the boys get top hats and Melanie a feathered tiara. Melanie and Kevin put theirs on.

Jeremy holds his hat upside down with one hand and, plunging his other hand all the way in and then out of it, announces, "Look what I can do! A rabbit!"

FEBRUARY 2002

saying words

About a year ago, we got into the habit of going around the table and saying thanks when we sit down to eat our supper.

Sometimes maybe two of the kids want to hold hands while we do it, but maybe the other one doesn't. Sometimes we make them all hold hands anyway, and sometimes we just work around it. It all depends.

Usually Jenny or I say something like, "We're happy and grateful to share this good food here together." The kids gave it a name. They call it saying words.

Pretty soon the kids wanted to make up their own words. For a long time, they would each think for a minute and then say, "Thanks for the dinner!" Or sometimes, "Thank you for everything, Mommy and Nana and Pop!" Whatever the first one said, they'd all say.

This winter, Kevin, age seven, got the idea of a moment of silence, instead. But the younger two still prefer words. So some nights we have a moment of silence—or something a little like silence—and then we have words.

Recently they've begun to think of new words. The other night Melanie said, "I wish for peace in the world and that all the bad guys will die." Jeremy said, "Yes, I hope all the bad guys die." Kevin chose silence that night, so after that we ate our dinner.

For Christmas, Jenny gave me a small book of comforting sayings, a few lines on each small page, a ribbon with a tiny key on the end to hold your place. Kevin found it on the kitchen shelf one evening, and now sometimes he likes to read his words from it. He thumbs through the pages with his marker-streaked hands while we're putting food on the plates, and he chooses one.

Tonight Kevin reads, "What is the perfect way to happiness? To stay at home."

For some reason, his five-year-old sister Melanie, who's known in the family for her kind and thoughtful ways, sticks her fingers in her ears and ostentatiously refuses to listen.

By the time Kevin finishes his reading, tears are running down his face.

"Kevin had a hard day," Jenny tells her. Melanie says she's sorry.

Jenny says to him, "Here, move over closer to me," and puts her arm around him. His tears stop, he eats up his meatballs and gets spaghetti sauce all over his face.

Near the end of dinner, Jeremy, age three, who had a big snack after school and left the table early, reappears in the kitchen doorway with a too-big straw hat on his head, swinging his arms like Groucho Marx, and circles the table once, chanting, "stinky, stinky, stinky, stinky."

After he leaves the room and then comes back in and does it again with a cardboard box on his head this time, everyone gets the giggles at dessert, including Kevin.

But Kevin is tired tonight.

Around eight, he asks me to put him to bed. "Rub my back," he says, under the covers. I start to rub his back. "Rub my shoulders, too. But not just my shoulders, rub all around."

I rub his neck and the back of his head. "Yes, that's good," he says, his eyes nearly closed. "Now say the words."

I say the bedtime words that we say every night—your feet are getting sleepy, your heels and your ankles, your knees, legs, back and shoulders, arms and hands, your head and your neck, and finally your eyes, so sleepy that they close, your whole body asleep all night long, until you wake up tomorrow morning, and your eyes open on a brand new day.

We're quiet for a minute before Kevin opens his eyes again and says, softly, sleepily, "I want to learn how to meditate. I want to learn how to sit for a long time. I want to know how to pray. I don't know the words to any prayers.

"I want to learn the words."

MARCH 2002

tonight's blessing

Tonight before supper, the kids turn out the kitchen light and find candles for the table. Kevin puts on his tape of the musical chant that he performed with his class last year.

When we sit down, I ask if we can all join hands. "Tonight let's go around the table," I say. "I'll start."

"We are thankful," I say.

"We are thankful," Kevin repeats.

"We are lucky," Jenny says.

"We are happy," Melanie says.

And Jeremy, who is three years old and later on that evening tells us he wants to change his middle name from David to Race Car Fruit Loops, says, "We are love. And peace in the world."

Let it be so.

APRIL 2002

birthday party at the soccerplex

Kevin wants to bring his origami book to his classmate Dylan's eighth birthday party at the soccerplex.

"You can't take origami with you when you're going to play soccer," I say.

"I need it!" he says. But he puts it away.

On the way over I say, "It's been a long time since you've played soccer."

"Yes," he says. "But there's one important thing I remember. Always kick the ball with the side of your foot."

When we get there, some of the other kids are already chasing the ball around the field. Dylan's mom opens the gate for Kevin. He looks at her. "What should I do?" he asks.

"Just go on in and start playing," she says.

He runs around with the other boys for a little while, until he notices that one of the goals is empty. He goes over to it and stands in front of the net.

A teenager comes in and organizes the kids into teams. Kevin isn't the goalie now, but he stays back near the goal for a few minutes before he starts racing around the field with the others.

And then, suddenly, he's kicking the ball whenever he can, even when other guys are trying to get it, too. Down near the end of the field, he kicks it hard and scores the first goal.

At time-out, one of the other boys is mad at Kevin for knocking him down during the game. "But I didn't even see you," Kevin says. "I was totally focused on the ball."

After lunch, that kid and some others start rough-housing. Kevin thinks they're fighting and tries to break it up. One of them gets him into a choke hold. I pull them apart. George puts his arm around him, and Kevin cries, but only a little. He stands with us a few minutes, watching some big kids play.

When they light the candles, he walks back to the table and sings Happy Birthday to Dylan. He waits his turn and then asks Dylan's mom if he can have a piece of cake with flowers on it.

Going home, I tell him how proud we were when he scored. "I wanted the other kids to be as happy as me," he says. "I want to play soccer in a real game, one that has a real scoreboard that shows who won."

MAY 2002

storytellers

Kevin, age seven, makes up a story tonight. It's two pages! The longest he's ever written!

Once upon a time, he dictates, there was a castle. And in the castle there lived a king, a queen, a prince and a princess. The castle was in a village. They had five hundred knights. But they didn't have any gardens. They didn't have any gardens because they didn't have any seeds. And they didn't have any seeds because they didn't have any boats. So they built a boat. But it didn't sail. So they tried again and built another boat. This one was much simpler, like a raft, and it floated. They sailed it all the way across the Pacific Ocean to America, which they'd never heard of because they'd never heard of Christopher Columbus. And luckily they brought things along in their pockets to trade with the Americans for seeds. They weren't exactly the kind of seeds they wanted, but they were happy, because they were vegetable seeds. And they wanted vegetables, because they'd only had meat to eat for twelve hundred years! And this all happened yesteryear! The End.

Later in the evening after the littler kids are put to bed, I remember there's going to be a documentary on TV about Mark Twain. "He was a storyteller," I tell Kevin.

"I want to watch with you," he says. "I'll take notes."

He scoots to get his big drawing pad from his shelf and sits down at the coffee table on one of the kid-size chairs. He uses a stencil to write MARK TWAIN in capital letters across the top of the page. Stomach cancer, he writes as they tell about the death of Clemens' father-in-law.

When they begin the story of a former slave woman who worked as a servant for the Clemens family, Kevin leans forward. A female voice speaks the words as if they're her own. She and her husband had seven children. One day, men came, and they took them all.

She held Henry, her youngest, tight, as he whispered to her, "Don't worry, Mama. I'll escape and earn a lot of money and buy your freedom." But they sold him, too.

Kevin looks up, eyes wide with disbelief. Then he hunches over, head down, clutching his hands between his knees.

I reach out my arms to him, and he climbs into my lap, holding tight, bending his skinny legs so he'll fit, but still listening as the woman's voice continues: years later, during the Civil War, she was working in North Carolina, when a regiment of black soldiers showed up and ordered her to get them some breakfast. Bending over the oven to pull out a tray of biscuits, she saw one of the men standing near her—her own Henry.

Kevin buries his head and tries not to cry, but it takes a while for him to stop the tears. He stands up. "Can I get a glass of water?" he asks.

"A little one," I say. "It's close to bed time."

"I know," he says. "It helps me control myself when I'm feeling bad." He takes a few sips.

"That feels better," he says.

And he sits back down at his pad and draws a small slave cabin at the very top of a hill, with a big star shining in the sky above it.

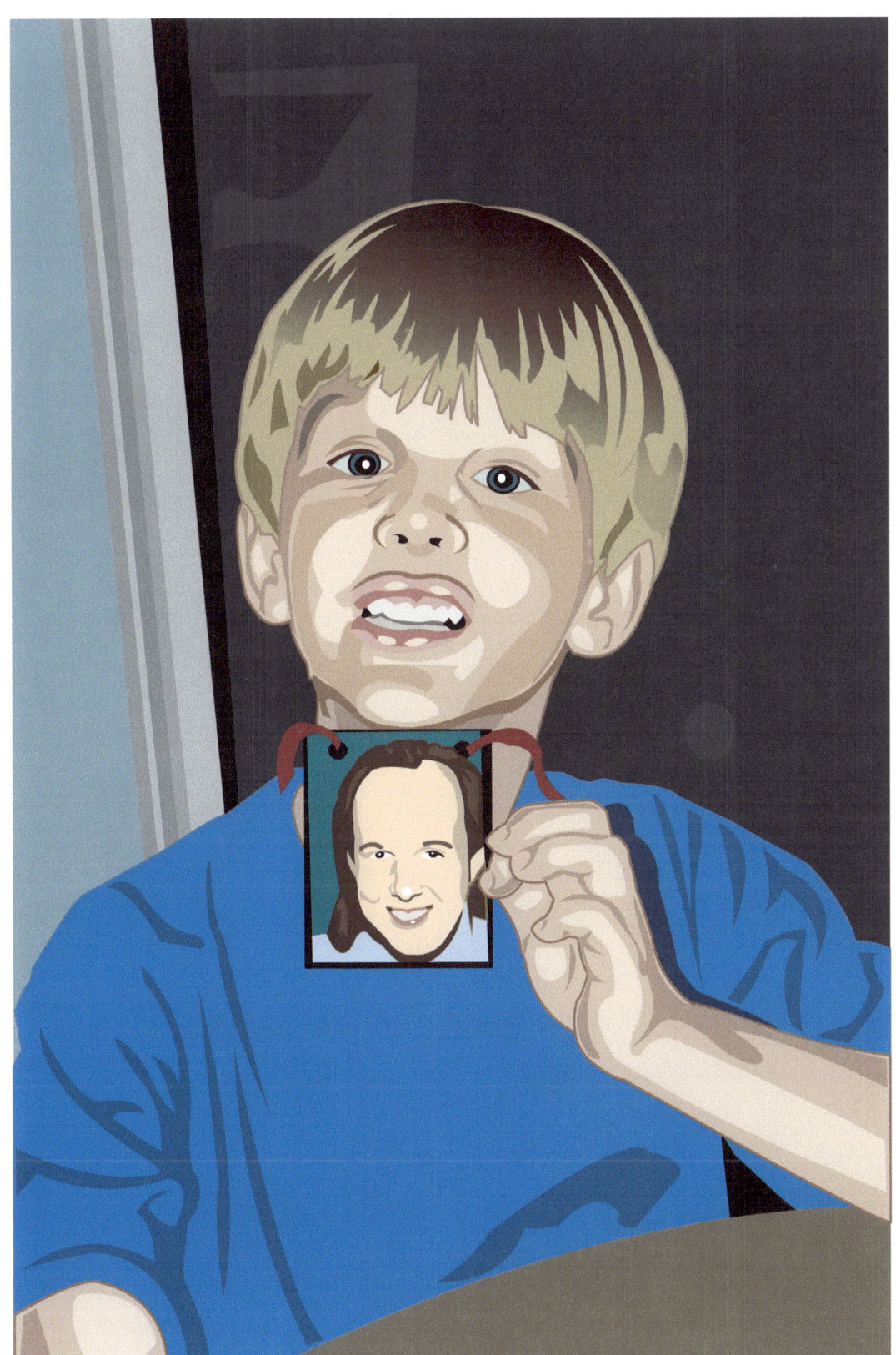

JUNE 2002

negotiation

After they've played hide-and-seek around the bedrooms and the living room for a half an hour or so, Jeremy tells Melanie he wants to play a different game.

"Okay," says Melanie. "Let's play dog. You be the owner, and I'll be the dog. I'll be your worker dog, and I'll pick berries for you."

Jeremy hesitates. "But I want to be the dog," he says.

"Okay," says Melanie. "I'll be the owner, and you be the dog. You'll have to be my worker dog and pick all the berries for me."

"Okay," says Jeremy.

"But," says Melanie, "I really want to be a dog."

"Arf!" says Jeremy.

"Arf! Arf!" says Melanie, and they gallop down the hall together on all fours.

AUGUST 2002

kindergarten girl

We have a kindergarten girl named Melanie in our house. She's five years old, and she can spell her own name and her brothers' names and "I Love You" completely by herself, with no helping at all. She can tell you how many syllables there are in any word you can think of, and she figured out on her own that bird, spelled backwards, is drib.

The comforter and pillowcases and sheets on Melanie's bed all have blue skies and white clouds on them, and so do Melanie's slippers and her favorite pajamas, which Melanie loves so much that sometimes she puts them on without even being told, before it's even time for supper, and she keeps wearing them even after she gets ketchup on the sleeves and never wants to put them in the laundry. If you say, "Melanie, you've got ketchup on your sleeves," Melanie just giggles.

One of Melanie's very favorite things is her pillowcase. Pillowcases, actually. Because she has four of them, all of them sky blue with white clouds. Melanie can think of a lot of things to do with her pillowcases. Like, you could wear one as a cape, or a skirt, or put some of your toys in it, or sometimes crawl inside one and pretend to be a turtle or a rabbit, hopping down the hall with your little brother in his own pillowcase with fire engines on it.

Or, if you want to bring something with you when you spend the night at someone else's house, you could bring your pillowcase. And at bedtime, of course, Melanie makes sure she has one near her pillow, just in case she needs to cuddle with it after we say good night.

Melanie's favorite colors are purple and pink and blue. She likes to eat strawberries and tomatoes and cheese and shrimp and blueberry blintzes and chocolate pudding.

Melanie would like to wear pajamas all day long. If you tell her she has to put some clothes on, she only wants to wear a skirt or a dress.

At the playground, Melanie can swing all the way across with her hands on the monkey bars. And she likes to climb up Pop's legs and somersault back down.

But if it's time to be quiet, Melanie says, "I know how to do that. Just listen to music and look out the window." And then she twirls a strand of her long straight hair with her right hand and sucks the thumb of her left, just the way she's done since she was very, very small.

When Melanie was one day old and she first came home from the hospital, her Daddy sat down cross-legged in the sunlight on the living room rug and watched his new baby girl as she slept in his arms.

Of course Melanie can't remember that. She was way too little. But she definitely remembers Daddy and how much she loved to cuddle in his lap, even though she can't do it anymore. He died when she was three. But Melanie still loves to cuddle.

In fact, I think that's what Melanie likes the very best. To cuddle, to sit on your lap and twirl her hair—maybe you could rub her shoulder a little bit, that feels good when you do that. Just like in the picture on her bedroom wall—Melanie sitting in Daddy's lap in the big rocking chair, both of their eyes closed, no need to talk. Just sitting there quietly, together.

MARCH 2003

melanie's questions

Tonight at bedtime, Melanie needs to talk.

"Today at school," she starts, and then her voice begins to shake. "My friend told me that she can only have one best friend in the world, and I'm not her best friend anymore!"

"Oh," I say to her. "You must have felt really sad. Your feelings must really have been hurt."

"Yes," she says, crying.

"You know," I say to her, "that happened to me when I was a kid. It happened more than once."

"Tell me about every time it happened to you," she says. "Tell me how old you were every time."

I tell her some ages—8, 12, 13, especially 13, 15, (21, 35, I'm thinking)—but she's only 5, and I stop at 15, hoping even these ages don't seem too old to console her.

She asks, "Did you ever have any fights with your friends? Tell me what friends you had fights with."

Well, okay. But it's a long time ago, and I don't even feel like trying to remember them. So I go with what's handy and say, "Well, you know, Pop and I have fights sometimes."

"What do you say when you fight?" she wants to know.

"Oh, something like—'You're wrong!' 'No, you're wrong!'"

"How do you stop being angry?" she asks.

"Well, one of us says, let's stop saying angry words. You listen to me, and I'll listen to you."

"Who stops saying angry words first?" she asks.

"It depends. Sometimes it's one, sometimes the other."

"But how can you tell when the fight is over?" she asks. "How do you know that you're sorry?

"How do you know you're not angry anymore?"

MAY 2004

jeremy thinks about the future

Jeremy's daddy died four days after Jeremy turned two. And ever since he's been able to form the thought, Jeremy has said, "I don't want to grow up. I'm not going to be a daddy. I want to be a kid forever."

If you ask him what he wants to be when he grows up, he usually answers, "I'm not going to grow up." A little while ago, when the subject came up again, I asked him softly, "Jeremy, are you afraid that daddies die?"

And Jeremy quietly replied, "Yes."

Still, I like to check in with him every now and then on his feelings about the future, when not too much else is going on. And this evening, a month before Jeremy's fifth birthday, while we're lying on the bed watching a road construction video before saying good night, I ask Jeremy if he'd like to learn to drive a bulldozer, and he says, "Yes. That would be cool. I want to be a construction man when I grow up."

And then he reconsiders and says he'd rather drive the giant dump trucks or maybe the roller, smoothing the asphalt.

After a while, pulling the quilt up to his chin and cuddling close, he says, "I changed my mind. I don't want to be a construction man because, you know, I get tired sometimes.

"I just want to be a plain dad. A dad and a teacher.

"And then, when one of the kids wants to play with the hamster, I'll go get it for him."

JUNE 2005

the shoe man's story

Kevin needs tennis shoes for fourth grade field day tomorrow, so I take him to Target, where, since there's never any service, prices are low.

We find the boys' shoes and begin the usual process of taking down boxes from the open racks, Kevin sitting on the floor trying on one pair after another and then walking around the aisles pigeon-toed—since each pair is tied together with white elastic string—when a short, older man in a red Target polo shirt walks over to us and stops.

But since everyone knows customers are on their own in the shoe department at Target, I assume this man is standing near us only by coincidence—he must actually be concerned with something else—until he says, "Those are too big."

"No they're not," says Kevin.

The man exhorts Kevin to try on a smaller pair, and though, after a trial walk, Kevin reports that they're tight, the Target shoe man asserts they're just right. "After two to three weeks, they'll fit perfectly," he says.

"But I have to wear them tomorrow!" says Kevin. "For four hours!"

"Well, wear good socks and pull them up," the man says, bending down on one knee to pull up Kevin's socks.

"They're tight!" says Kevin.

I thank the Target shoe man for his valuable advice and tell Kevin we can look at some other pairs before we decide.

Kevin's feet are right between boy-size and man-size right now, and there aren't a lot of choices, so it takes us a while to find anything else that fits, and Kevin's trying on a big blue pair when the shoe man reappears beside us.

He sticks his index finger down the heel of the shoe Kevin's wearing and says, "These are too big."

"They're perfect," says Kevin.

"Try the smaller size," says the shoe man, and Kevin puts them on and makes his circuit around the department.

"Too tight," he says when he returns.

"Well," says the shoe man, "don't worry. They will stretch in two to three weeks. Those are good shoes, tough. No bugs can bite through them, or even snakes!" He reaches up to the top shelf of the rack and takes down another pair—white leather high-tops—in the larger size Kevin prefers.

"These shoes are tough, too. Good to wear in the woods. No snakes can bite through these." And while Kevin tries them on, the Target shoe man tells us his story.

"There was a snake in my house when I grew up," he says. "It had its own room. It lives there still and has long gray whiskers. This was in India.

"My father was a barrister, a very successful man, and when I was five years old and my brother was a baby, my father had a cerebral hemorrhage at the court and died. My mother was a widow and she said to me, 'It's up to you now. You must study hard and become a barrister and carry on.' And I did. I am a barrister."

Kevin completes his lap around the racks of shoes and squats near us on the floor in the white leather high-tops. He looks up at the Target shoe man and doesn't say a word.

"But when I was small," says the man, "one night, the snake came out of his room and nudged me awake. I got up and stood against the wall. The snake, it was a cobra, reared up like this," and he raises his forearm and bends his wrist so that his hand and arm form an upside-down U.

"But he didn't attack. He just crossed to the other side of the room and reared up once more. And then he slithered out the window and over the roof to go hunting. And he did that every night and returned to his room every morning.

"No one ever went into the snake's room except to clean. Every day, we mixed cow dung with water and washed the snake's room. Do you know what cow dung is?"

I nod.

"And every night we spread butter in his room and lit candles. And the snake never bothered us. We believe that hundreds of years ago someone buried gold coins and gold belts underneath that room, and the snake is the spirit guarding the gold. We are Hindus, you know," he says, "and our mythology tells us that snakes are good spirits. If you don't attack a snake, it won't attack you.

"I sent my son to the United States to get an education, and now I am an old man, and he has sent for me, and I am here, and the snake is still in the house. And I think that is the way it is supposed to be."

I thank the shoe man for sharing his story and say it's time for us to go. But he has a little more to tell us. "Have you ever been to Safari Canada?" he asks.

"There are many tigers there. I walked peacefully among rows and rows of tigers, and they just looked at me. If you don't attack tigers, they won't attack you."

Kevin keeps the white leather high-tops on and wears them home.

NOVEMBER 2005

not full yet

Kevin takes some books along in the car to keep from getting bored on our errands.

"*How Things Work*," he says from the back seat. "This will be good. It will help me figure out how to make my time machine."

He worked on his Electro Wizard kit for a couple of hours on Sunday. "Okay," he said to himself, "Okay," touching wires to batteries, until the 9-volt battery got hot, and he figured he'd better give it a rest.

Monday evening, when Jenny walked into his room and saw that he'd taken a tape recorder apart, he said, "Don't worry. I won't take apart anything we use, like a lamp."

Tonight we all go out to dinner. George and the two boys want meat, so Jenny and Melanie and I bring our vegetarian burritos to the cheeseburger joint, where the boys sit waiting in a big booth for their meals.

Jeremy's ordered the chicken strips that get served in a cardboard convertible. Kevin's ordered an apple pie shake and a half-pound burger, the one so big that, if a kid can eat it, the waitress will take a picture of him and put it on the wall.

"I can eat it," he says. "I deliberately didn't order any fries."

"Take it easy with the milkshake," we warn him. And even though he doesn't really want to, he passes it around the table to let everyone have a taste, even his little brother Jeremy, just this once.

Dinner arrives.

Kevin's burger is as big as a dessert plate, its rough brown edges sagging over the sides of the bun. He takes big bites, wiping his hands with the napkins we urge on him, pausing for lumpy drags on the shake through his straw. When he stuffs the last of it into his mouth, he looks up, grinning with his lips closed, eyes wide, his cheeks puffed out and shiny with grease, still chewing.

We flag down the waitress. She brings over her Polaroid. Kevin gets up and stands next to a 6-foot cardboard cutout of Speed Racer. The camera whirs, and the picture slides out through its slot.

The waitress hands it to him with a pen, and he sits back down in the booth and holds the picture by the corner as the image forms.

"Will you take the cap off the pen for me?" he asks. "My fingers are too greasy."

So we pass him another napkin, and in turquoise ink, in letters small enough to fit on the white Polaroid border, he writes:

Kevin Lyons (I'm not full yet)

jean

OCTOBER 2001

keepsakes

My mother-in-law Jean has found some things to share with us when George and I stop by at her assisted living place.

Just like in the old days

she's managed yet again to rearrange the furniture we brought from her house when she moved here last spring.

And she's scissored out a picture from the newspaper, black and white, three columns wide, a baby elephant nuzzling behind its mother's stolid legs, the baby's eyes timid, dark and round.

"So tender," she says, her eyes full, both hands pressing the paper tight to her chest.

Sometimes these days

Jean uncovers a memory from years ago, fresh from storage, never spoken.

"I was just thinking," she tells us, "When my dad was my age now, he never wanted to leave his house, never even wanted to take vacation. Just the same, my brothers and I arranged a trip to Florida. I was the one who took him. We went to the ocean, to the beautiful beach.

"But Dad just sat there with his arms folded, staring straight ahead. He wouldn't even talk until we got back home.

"Me, I'd travel anywhere. I could even pick up and leave this place and live somewhere else if I had to.

"It's just the way I am.

"Isn't that good?"

JANUARY 2002

this week at the doctors' with jean

Jean's toe is sore.

It hurts like crazy, she tells me on the phone on Friday. I tell her we'll ask the cardiologist about it when we see him on Monday.

She says, "I think it has something to do with my, my—"

"Circulation?"

"That's it! Why can't I ever remember that?" I tell her I think she might be right.

On Monday

Jean's foot still hurts a lot, so I drop her off at the door of the medical building before parking the car.

Inside, the nurse is unsmiling. She tells Jean to strip to the waist, put on the paper vest and remove her socks and shoes. When the cardiologist comes in, Jean tells him she's turned 85 and gives him a hug. He asks if she's had any problems.

"No," she says.

I say, "Your foot?"

She says, "Oh, yes, my foot," and shows it to him.

"Ouch!" she says when he touches it. "Watch it!"

He says it might be her circulation, it could turn into gangrene. He refers us to a vascular surgeon.

But we remember how, last summer, the last time Jean went to see the vascular surgeon, the operation turned out to be harder than they'd predicted, and Jean hated being in the hospital, and she felt confused and angry, and it took a week before she even wanted to eat again. So George and I decide to try Jean's regular doctor first this time.

On Thursday morning

when I get to the assisted living place, Jean's still in her room.

She's got a guest—Vicki, a new resident. Vicki just moved in last week from Philadelphia to be near her daughter, but she's not adjusted yet. She had hip surgery recently and can't make her own bed, and the furniture they have here for her, it's just not right.

I touch Jean on the shoulder. "Well, dear, I've got to go," Jean tells her.

As she gets up to leave, Vicki catches her reflection in Jean's mirror. "Oh, my. I look like I'm 105 years old," she says.

"Well, you know, dear," Jean says. "We're all old."

Jean's neighbor, Audrey, is making her way down the hall in a pastel flowered housedress, leaning on her walker. In the lobby she stands and watches as we go through the double doors and then calls out, "We're going to have Bible study!"

Jean, halfway out, leans back inside. "What?" she calls.

"We're going to have Bible study right here!" calls Audrey.

"Well, I have to go to the doctor," calls Jean.

At the doctor's office

the nurse weighs Jean when we arrive. "108 pounds. That's just about right!" says Jean.

"She's spunky," says the nurse.

The doctor comes in and takes Jean's left foot in her hands. She says it's not infected, the circulation's not too bad, but Jean should see a podiatrist. "Jean doesn't have a podiatrist," I say.

"I'll call the one in this building," says the doctor. "I've done him some favors, now he can do one for me."

Minutes later

a smiling, chubby man appears in the podiatrist's waiting room and props the door open. When we go into the examining room, we discover that he's the doctor.

"How are you doing?" he asks Jean.

"Well, my foot hurts. But I'm okay. I'm 85."

"Eighty-five?" he says. "Then you can do anything you want. My dad's 74, and you put him to shame."

Jean laughs. He examines her foot. "Ouch!" she says.

"I don't see any infection," he says. "But let's take an x-ray and see if there's anything hiding under the skin."

He goes out. Jean and I look at the diagrams of feet on the wall. We're both amazed at how long the toe bones are and comment on it at length.

The nurse arrives with brown paper slippers for Jean's feet. "Careful!" Jean says as the nurse leads her out the door. A few minutes later, Jean returns with a smile on her face.

"This is great," she says.

The nurse snaps two x-rays into the light box on the wall. The podiatrist stands pondering them for a minute. "Well, my dear," he says to Jean, "No wonder your foot is hurting you. You have a broken toe!"

"Well, for heaven's sake," says Jean.

He tapes Jean's little toe to the one next to it and writes her a prescription for penicillin, just to be on the safe side. Jean puts on her socks and shoes. On the way out, we make an appointment to come back next week.

"It feels better already!" Jean says. She's beaming.

"And just think," she says as we walk to the car, "We'll be back home in time for lunch! I saw the chef working in the kitchen this morning, and I know he was up to something good!"

Back at her place

Jean walks ahead of me. Inside, lunch has apparently just ended. Ladies with walkers are rolling out of the dining room toward us. One of them waves. "What did the doctor say?" she asks me.

"She's got a broken toe," I say.

She looks at Jean. "How'd you do it?"

Jean raises her eyebrows and her hands and laughs.

"I don't know!" she says.

Vicki approaches. "What did the doctor say?" she asks.

"Well, it ain't broke!" says Jean.

"Yes it is," I say.

"Oh, yes," says Jean. "I've got a broken toe!"

She makes her way past the other ladies into the dining room. One of the women from the table next to hers is still there, snoozing over her half-empty plate.

Jean stops at the serving counter and leans into the kitchen. "Hi there!" she says. "Got anything left for me?"

She hangs her coat over the back of her chair and sits down. One of the guys from the kitchen brings her a plate of ravioli and buttered Italian bread and then a cup of tea.

"I wish I could tell you to pull up a chair and have something to eat with me," she says when I lean to kiss her good-bye. "Here. At least have a bite of my bread."

"It's so good," she says. "Still warm."

APRIL 2002

stuart and francine

Today

Jean has to go to the doctor again, still her foot, slow to heal, not surprising in an eighty-five-year-old with iffy circulation. But it's bringing us back to her smiling podiatrist once a week or so.

They like her there. The nurse calls her Perky, even though Jean's foot is bothering her so much these days that she's getting around very slowly with the help of a cane lent to her by Audrey, who lives next door.

Jean was voted Miss Congeniality in high school, McKinley Tech, Class of '34. And even with Jean's cane, the nurse is right. Perky is the word for her, in her black stirrup pants, with her flowered silk scarf knotted in a fat bow.

"I'm going to study the way you go," she tells me every time we set off. "I think I've been on these roads sometime before, but I have no idea where we are now!"

Still, you shouldn't be fooled. The roads may be a mystery to her, but Jean remembers a lot.

Like the time in the '40s when

Jean and her first husband, Al, and their little boy, Allen Jr., lived in a house on High Castle Circle with Al's older brother, Stuart, who died young, and Stuart's beautiful wife, Francine.

Wait a minute. Stuart and Francine? Years of Sunday afternoons spent reminiscing with us, and Jean's never even mentioned these names before. Is there more?

"Well," says Jean, "You know, Al was a gambler, and money was tight." And when their apartment rent got to be too much, the house on High Castle Circle seemed like the best place to go. Stuart and Francine already lived there, and besides, it was owned by Al's father, a stern man who had only one arm, though he did everything for himself, even drove his own car. Jean gave him a lot of credit for that.

"Well, you know Al was fun and kind of rough," she says. "But Stuart was a priss. When you walked into a room where Stuart was sitting, he acted as if you didn't deserve to breathe the same air."

And Francine? Well, Francine was a sorority girl, tall, with beautiful red-blonde hair and a great figure. Jean knew girls like Francine in high school. Some of them were nice. But most looked down their noses at you. Francine was like that.

There was one thing about Francine, though. She had a deep scar on her forehead, marks from a difficult birth, back in 1916. "She must have been hard to bear," says Jean.

When Al left to join the Army, Jean stayed on with Stuart and Francine, even though she never felt at home in that house. Finally, sick of Al's gambling debts and lonely, too, she decided to get a divorce.

And here's the part we already know by heart.

How, desperate to get away from High Castle Circle, she'd asked her father if she could move back home and bring her son, Allen, with her, and he'd told her no—"You've made your bed, now lie in it." How after that, she'd found a room to rent from a woman she'd known in school, Sissy Koontz, and her husband, Harold, who were childless and took in lodgers.

How, later, Jean started making enough money to rent a real apartment for herself and her little boy. How, after she and Al were divorced, he started picking their son up for afternoon visits now and then. And how, on one of those visiting days, without a word, Al just didn't bring Allen back—ever.

But that's a whole other story. And a very long one.

And anyway, for now, Jean's busy finishing every last bite of the Southwest Salad she's ordered for lunch on the way home from the doctor, admiring her salad bowl made of a red tortilla, and how its shape makes her think of a rose.

MAY 2002

tornado warning

Two weeks ago

Jean had another heart attack—she was discovered on the floor of her room by Clive, the head cook, after he went in to see what was up when he missed her smiling face at breakfast that morning.

Jean loves Clive. He knows just how she likes her oatmeal, not runny. He brings Red Delicious apples, the ones she likes best, to her room in the afternoons, the only room in the whole house completely furnished with her own things from home—her two round sky-blue chairs, little, like she is, her blue-flowered slipcovers tucked snugly around her old love seat, the lacy blue comforter that she ordered from the Penney's catalog last June spread across her bed, and the matching lacy blue valance hung above her big bay window—with the help of Clive, after she first moved here last year, after her second heart attack.

This time

Jean lies in the green-painted ICU for five days, hooked up to all the usual monitors, their canyons and peaks tracing across the screen above her head, Jean asking us over and over,

"Where are we?

"What got me to this place?"

One night she imagines her bed is a bus driving down Pennsylvania Avenue to the movies. "You two are so good," she says to us when we walk into her darkened room, "I knew you'd find me, even if I was all the way downtown."

Saturday night

they move her to a regular hospital room, to a bed not near the window, a room with walls painted a pinkish peach, the pink plaid curtain between the beds always drawn, separating Jean from the lady on the window side,

Adele, who's had back surgery and moans in pain, her younger relatives arriving in shifts wearing tee shirts labeled Team Adele, milling in and out past Jean's bed.

Still, Jean seems livelier almost from the moment she arrives there, more like her old chatty self.

Thursday

we drive Jean from the hospital over to the nursing home next door to her assisted living place.

"One step closer to home," she says.

Her feet are tender and sore, her legs so weak now that she can't stand up at all. So the taciturn nursing assistant buckles her into a green canvas sling without explanation and hoists her through the empty air, terrified, to be weighed.

"Watch the feet!" Jean cries, now officially ninety-eight pounds, nine pounds lighter than she was a week ago.

Even so, she says, "What a beautiful room!" once she's safely tucked under her white bed covers, next to a big double window.

"I love this window," she says,

"I love that red rooftop out there and the sky and the tops of the trees."

And when I lean down to kiss her good-bye and say to her, "I hate to leave you," she says, "I'll be okay. I'm where I need to be."

We'd planned a trip, the three of us, Jean, George and me, for that weekend.

"I think you'll have to go without me," Jean tells us after her heart attack. "But take my new suitcase along! At least it can go with you!"

Late Sunday afternoon

when George and I get back from our trip, Jean is sitting in a wheelchair by the window, head slumped forward, cheeks hollow, thinner even than she was when we left.

George hooks up the video he made for her while we were away, and Jean waves at the TV when someone on the screen waves to her, but other times, she says, "This is so boring. Why doesn't somebody turn that thing off?" And sometimes she just closes her eyes.

Monday afternoon

George and I drive over to the nursing home to talk with Jean about what might happen next, to help her sign her advance directive, her living will—resuscitate, do not resuscitate, heroic measures or none.

And here's Jean, her head down, her wheelchair again parked facing the wall next to the bed.

Still, as soon as she hears George's voice, she looks up at him and grins. "Oh, my!" she says. "How did you ever get here? I am so glad to see you!"

We wheel her into a small sitting room, past the line-up of confused women in wheelchairs stationed along the wall near the nurses, so we can talk, so she can say once more the things she's said to us so many times before.

"I love my life," she's told us both over the years. "But don't think I want to live to be 100. I just want to live as long as I'm enjoying it."

Once she gave us a brochure from the Hemlock Society about dying with dignity. "I just want to drift away," she said.

And last month in the car one sunny morning she said to me, "I've lived a good life. I've lived a bad life. And I've lived everything in between. So don't think I'm afraid to die. Because I'm not."

This time, though

there are papers to sign, lines to check off or cross out or initial. This time Jean has to listen slowly.

"Just a minute," she says, and closes her eyes while George waits until her thoughts have caught up with her.

"Okay," she nods, and he continues. "Okay. That's right."

The head nurse has more questions for Jean before agreeing to witness her signature. She looks into Jean's eyes as she speaks, finally satisfied that Jean understands what she's about to sign.

And then

just as Jean picks up the pen to sign the final line, the nurse turns her head. "I need to listen to this," she says.

It's the loudspeaker: "Everyone away from the windows!" it crackles. "Tornado warning!"

I wheel Jean into the hall as George helps the nurses and the aides negotiate wheelchairs and hospital beds through doorways to line them up along the walls, an obstacle race in slow-motion.

"George! I'm thirsty!" one of the ladies calls to him.

"I'm sorry, I have to go help my mom now," he tells her.

"But George," she cries, "I'm thirsty!"

By the time all the rooms have been emptied, the warning is lifted. "Let's just give them their snacks in the hall," one of the aides calls out.

George hands Jean his pen.

"What are we doing with this?" she asks him.

"Just write your initials here, Mom," he says. "Remember?"

The head nurse passes us. "Just let me know," she says. "I'll sign it when you're done."

George goes to make photocopies. I wheel Jean back to her room, threading her wheelchair between the beds and other wheelchairs that still line both sides of the hall. It's a tight squeeze, but we make it without bumping anybody.

A woman in one of the beds nods to us. "Well done," she says. Another woman in a wheelchair smiles and claps her hands.

The next day

when we get there and I say good morning to her, Jean smiles at me for a minute and then asks, "Who are you?" And the day after that, she doesn't seem to remember either of our names.

But when I walk into her room on Thursday, she throws open her arms and calls, "There's my Susie!"

It turns out

there actually was a tornado that afternoon, but it touched down well to the north. We saw it in the paper Tuesday morning.

We were never really in danger, even though the clouds turned that stormy greenish color and the rain pelted the ground in sheets, and the treetops outside Jean's window shook and swayed.

JUNE 2002

wednesday afternoon with jean in her hospice room

The door to Room 7 is closed, and Jean is sleeping when I come in, her head drooping off the pillow to her left. I bring over a pillow from the window seat, wedge it under her shoulder and then add another, a blue frilly one from her old living room, just to be sure she's steady.

I sit down by the bed, watch her breathe.

Judy, the nursing aide, comes in. "What can you tell me today?" I ask her.

She sits on the chair across the bed from me and, in her Trinidadian lilt, describes Jean's breakfast—yogurt, jello and juice, eaten late, not until 11:00—and how well Jean tolerated her bathing afterward.

"Lift the sheet," she tells me, pointing out the big sponge on which they've propped Jean's legs, to keep her heels from rubbing against the mattress.

"What a great idea," I say.

"I see her smile in her sleep," Judy says. "That means she's getting happiness from the ones she's meeting on her journey. She smiles when she talks to them."

"That's how she's lived her life," I say.

Eyes closed, deep inside herself, Jean nods twice. "She hears us," I say.

"We're not important to her anymore," says Judy. "It's just her journey that matters to her now."

Judy leaves.

I turn on the tape we brought over when we cleared Jean's things out of her assisted living room last weekend. It's a tape I gave her years ago, my grandma, Gus, playing the piano—Gus, whose piano played through all the summers of my childhood, weaving with the breeze through her windows as we rocked, reading, in the hammock outside and up the stairs at night to the bedrooms, where it blended with the rhythms of the crickets in the dark—the same songs playing here on this tape for my dreaming mother-in-law, Jean, who's raising her head, lifting her good left ear from her old blue pillow. Her eyes are closed, but I think she's listening. I think she's feeling the music.

Jean's mother, she's told me so many times, always tenderly and with regret, yearned for her to become a concert pianist, so Jean took lessons for nine years and babysat for the piano teacher's three children to pay for them.

"But I never had the talent she thought I had," Jean always said, though she did always love the piano.

And now she lifts her chin, raises her brow, moves her head slowly on the pillow from side to side and smiles a few seconds as my grandma, Gus, dead for nearly ten years, plays for Jean and me—daughters, mothers, grandmothers mingling in this music in this quiet corner room—this late May afternoon.

While outside through Jean's window, the lawn guys, tan shirt tails billowing, are riding their mowers like chariots, crisscrossing the grassy hillside in speeding arcs, heads back, hair blowing, laughing.

And down the hallway from us, a man's voice calls, "See you later, Mom. Okay. Bye. See you later."

Here in Room 7, Gus is playing Schumann. I picture her, head bowed toward the keys, face intent, arms powerful, fingers swift.

While, her eyes still closed tight, Jean, on her pillows, on her journey, smiles.

home

MARCH 2002

signs of spring

Ahhh, at last, a few days dark and raw with rain, after this ridiculously warm winter, temperatures popping up as relentlessly as a demented jack-in-the-box. At least that's the way it felt to me.

The wiper blade on the driver's side of the station wagon is shot, squeegeeing the top and bottom of the windshield, but leaving a wide arc of puddled drops across the middle undisturbed. George tried replacing the blade the other day, but the bolt was stuck and he cut his hand, we were late, and he was getting rained on.

I stay in the car a few extra minutes after I get back this wet morning to listen to a song on the radio. The dogs see me through the window when I get to the door and jump down from the couch and the big arm chair, their tails thumping hopefully on the rugs. I walk in. Okay, all right, good dogs.

Melanie picked our first crocus last Thursday and put it in a purple cup filled with water, where it wilted while she slept. Peering at it the next morning she said, "Well, at least it's still floating."

And yesterday afternoon when I called my mother-in-law and asked her how she was feeling, she answered, "I'm undergoing a metamorphosis."

It's been gray and rainy for five days, periwinkle spreading purply across the garden, daffodils popping dependably through the leaves, the forsythia bush rioting at the end of the driveway.

On the kitchen window sill, the amaryllis blossom that's about to open is so tall this time, it's almost touching the ceiling.

And my mother and father, who both turned eighty this winter, remember eating breakfast together the morning of their wedding day at Nedick's lunch counter in Los Angeles on the corner of Hollywood and Vine, 1948, fifty-four years ago to the day this day, the first day of spring.

MARCH 2002

edible flowers

I'm floating along in the stream of consciousness this blue morning, walking through the parking lot at Congressional Plaza—the same shopping center where we went for groceries with my mother when we were kids, before they'd even heard of rye bread here in Rockville. (My grandma Mollie would bring it in brown-stained paper bags with bagels from the Lower East Side of New York when she came to visit.)

I'm walking toward the grocery store to get the stuff I need to make spaghetti tonight, when a gust of wind grazes my face. And out of the blue, this thought appears, so clear I actually see the letters in the morning air: "I'm glad to be alive."

It takes me by surprise—this epiphany in a parking lot. Like violets blooming through rocks or lightning in snow, rainbows in clear skies, or edible flowers—which, it turns out, along with rye bread and bagels, bird-friendly coffee and organic spaghetti sauce, you can buy right here at Congressional Plaza, on the rack between the basil and the oregano.

Right here in Rockville. This place where, growing up, I felt so out of place that I swore I'd leave it forever and never look back. Poetry, painting, music, romance—the future I longed for, I was sure, wasn't here.

But here I am. Just up the road from Rockville, back where I started from. In a house with murals on the walls and a shady front yard—and spaghetti with flowers for supper tonight.

MARCH 2002

passover stories

We're having Passover tonight at Mom's house, like we do every year. Today it's Good Friday, and the kids are home from school. Jenny's tired and sleeping late, it's a day off for her, too, and the kids are milling in and out of my office in the basement.

Melanie

In the afternoon, I tell Melanie, our kindergartner, "We have to get dressed up. We're having Passover dinner tonight at Baba's house." She's been lying on the rug, drawing. She looks up at me thoughtfully. "Oh," she says. "So I guess that means we must be Jewish."

The young moms

Two of Jenny's friends, sisters, also young moms with little kids, come over while I'm getting dressed. They're all in the back yard, kids hanging off the swing set, when I go out to say hello. One of the women tells us that the husband of a friend of hers is Jewish, and her friend had to go with him to her in-laws' for Passover this week, even though she didn't want to. "She's Catholic," she says, as if that explains it. "But I guess Passover's an important holiday if you're Jewish, right?"

"It's a big one," I say.

Kevin

A few weeks ago Kevin, who's in second grade, told someone he's Jewish. "But you don't have to do anything if you're Jewish," he said. "You just have to be it." And it's easy to see where he got that idea because, actually, we go to a Unitarian church. And actually, the first night of Passover was the day before yesterday, even though we're having our seder tonight, so the kids wouldn't have to stay up late in the middle of the week.

Jean

Around 5:00 I drive over to pick up Jean, my mother-in-law, at the assisted living place where she's lived since last May. She's an old hand now, this is her tenth seder, but at first it was all new to her. "We had only one Jewish boy in our school, growing up," she says. "Though I imagine they had more in New York."

Jean hasn't been feeling very well lately, but she's looking forward to Passover tonight, and she's brought along a bottle of bubbly that someone or other gave her for her eighty-fifth birthday last month—she'll never drink it, why shouldn't somebody enjoy it—to give to Mom and Dad.

Seder

It's not a big group tonight, just us regulars, plus Lili, a friend of ours who works at the office with George.

As always, instead of the Haggadah, we read what Mom's written, enough xeroxed copies handed around so that everybody has one to read—Mom's version of the old story illustrated by Ethan, our nephew, when he was 11, retold in words the kids can follow.

Dad speaks first about peace and freedom and remembering those we love, as Kevin, impatient to read aloud, this year his first time ever, shuffles his pages.

He and Melanie take turns asking the four questions, both of them listening wide-eyed through the story of the baby Moses and the miraculous escape of the slaves, as Jeremy, just three, fidgets, impatient for supper. When it comes, he digs hungrily into the charoset, the matzoh, the hard-boiled egg, even the gefilte fish.

By the time they've finished their matzoh ball soup, the kids are all stunned to learn there'll be more to eat tonight before they can have their dessert, three little boxes of chocolate, one for each, brought for them by Lili, well worth the wait.

In fact we're all a little stunned by the quantity of food we've consumed. So the grown-ups wait for our dessert as Jenny gets the three chocolate-faced kids rounded up and into the car, and then we all go into the living room for coffee and pie and another Passover story, this one told by Lili.

Lili

This story begins in May of 1940, in Brussels, where Lili, 13 that year, lived with her parents and her 16-year-old sister, and where it had gotten very clear to them that life was only going to get more and more dangerous.

Lili's father, a diamond broker, had narrowly escaped getting caught in a roundup of Jewish men near his office. And with her blond and blue-eyed sister and all those German soldiers in the streets—who knew what could happen?

So her father bought identification papers for all four of them, plus Lili's grandfather, and they started walking toward Paris, fifteen miles a day, the grandfather wearing his heavy winter coat in May, walking with many others, until they ran into the Battle of Dunkirk and had to turn around and flee back home, where by January, Lili's father had come up with another plan.

This time Lili's grandfather refused to leave. (She told us later he'd survived the war in Brussels, hidden in a room, nobody bothering with the old man, and after it was over the family brought him to New York, where he rented a room of his own and refused to live with them; they weren't religious enough. But that's getting ahead of the story.)

So this time, Lili's father got them train tickets to Paris and papers authorizing them to travel there on holiday. The train from Berlin to Paris boarded at Brussels around midnight, the kind of train you see now only in movies, with rows of compartments for eight that you entered from a long passageway. Most of the compartments were only partially filled, but no one would allow Lili's family to join them, so they sat on their suitcases against the wall in the long, cold, rattling corridor of the railway car.

After a while, Lili's mother opened the door to one of the compartments and, in her perfect German, she asked the passengers seated there if her girls could please be allowed to sit down and rest—they were so tired; it was the middle of the night.

Two of the passengers were German soldiers, and the one who looked older motioned that the girls could sit, and she and her husband could come in, too. Lili's mother sat in the seat next to the soldier, and as the night wore on, they chatted in German, the soldier telling her that he didn't believe in war and wished only to be back home with his family.

Then there was a knock at the door. Officials appeared, demanding everyone's papers. Lili's father knew little German. He mostly spoke Yiddish. Even after living in Belgium almost all his life, he'd never replaced his Polish passport with a Belgian one.

So when the officials demanded to see it, he mumbled in as few German words as possible that he'd misplaced it, it must be in his suitcase, which he opened and began rifling through for what seemed like forever to Lili, who couldn't understand why he didn't just give the men his passport. Why was it taking him so long to find it?

Finally, the older soldier raised his hand toward the officials, motioning them to move on. "They're all right," he told them.

And they continued to Paris.

In Paris, Lili's family stayed in a hotel with her aunt and uncle, like her father a diamond broker, who had hidden his diamonds in a can of condensed milk, until it exploded all over the room, and the whole family had to clean bits of diamonds and milk from the ceiling, the furniture and the walls, while they waited for passage by boat to Nicaragua. Each boat that left, they were told, was the last. And Paris was becoming more dangerous now, so Lili's father arranged with the Underground for the family to be smuggled into Free France.

But on the day they were to leave, Lili came down with an attack of appendicitis. A doctor was summoned and told her parents she had to stay in bed for three days. On the third day, the family got word there was space for them on a boat to Nicaragua, and they took it.

It was no ocean liner, not really even a large ship, but Lili and her sister were lucky to have a small cabin to themselves near their parents, luckier than some of the others who were crowded together on the lower decks, especially a few days out to sea when the sky got black and the boat started to rock on the gigantic waves, and suddenly amid the clatter of breaking dishes and the groans of the ship itself, the whole boat rolled completely to one side, then righted itself and rolled completely to the other side, before righting itself again, forcing the captain to bring it back to port in France, until the storm subsided and they could set off again.

Lili had an uncle who lived in New York, and her father wired him from the ship that he'd decided they should disembark when they docked in Cuba, instead of continuing all the way to Nicaragua. As they neared the harbor, Lili could see her uncle in a row boat, waving to them from the water below.

Once off the ship, all the new arrivals were herded into an internment area, which, with her uncle's help, Lili's family was able to leave after a few weeks. But nothing he did could make it possible for them to return with him to New York.

Pearl Harbor had happened just two months before, and nobody wanted more refugees. Or maybe, Lili's father thought, his brother had just made the wrong person mad or neglected some parking tickets.

Whatever it was, they were stuck in Cuba, not that Lili minded. She went to school and swam and rode her bicycle and learned Spanish and English with a British accent, until the war was over in 1945, and they finally made it to New York, America, to safe harbor, to new life. Not the promised land exactly, since it never had been promised to them. But certainly deliverance through the dark, dangerous nights to freedom, to peace, to possibility, over on the other shore.

JUNE 2002

watering the plants

Watering

Not hydrating, moistening, dampening, soaking, or even wetting. Putting water into. Watering. What better way to say it?

Planting

That's another one of those words that just plain says what it means. Rooting a plant in the dirt. We don't piano the piano or food our food. But we plant. And we water.

I'm watering the plants in our garden, spraying water from the green hose into the humid June afternoon. As the arcing droplets dapple their leaves, I'm sure my plants are breathing "aaaahhh" in grateful relief. The zinnias and impatiens are flowering. The hydrangeas—my sweethearts—are fat and delicate, lavender and indigo. My tender tomato plants are inching taller, exhaling tomato fragrance. The black-eyed susans promise to bloom soon.

And the round-leafed geranium that I planted this month in memory of my mother-in-law, Jean, who always had pots of red geraniums on her front stoop, has sprouted its first fire-engine red geranium flower.

Over us all

our immense oak's muscular branches weave in wide circumference, like the arms of a Hindu goddess. Climbing ivy clinging to its barky sides, it stands notwithstanding heat, cold, time, gravity, the leaping of hysterical squirrels, the incessant yearnings of the house creatures down below.

Older than everything around it, this tower of a tree draws our eyes to the sky and shelters the ground with green shade.

OCTOBER 2002

sniper

There's a sniper out there!

I'm driving in our old car, the station wagon whose front-door upholstery was clawed off by our dog when the car was new, and the dog was a puppy, and we left her in there for just a few minutes on a chilly day in May that was pouring rain.

And today, ten years or so later, while I'm driving to get some dog chow at the Safeway for our ten-year-old dog, my heart is pounding.

Because, even though you probably wouldn't know it to look at me, my heart knows that I'm thinking about what part of the Safeway parking lot will be least exposed to a direct shot from this sniper who, last night, killed a woman with a single bullet to her head, as she and her husband loaded packages into their car, parked at a Home Depot a few highway exits down from us—the ninth person he's killed around here in two weeks.

The other day, it actually crossed my mind that parking in the garage at the Home Depot near our house might possibly be a safe strategy, don't ask me why now.

This time last fall, some psycho was sending envelopes of anthrax here to Washington. That was scary. And not so different in some ways from this.

Scared of the mail. Scared of walking across the parking lot to the Safeway.

Hoping to be lucky enough to figure out a safe way into the grocery store.

Walking fast from the car.

Breathing a sigh of relief when I make it, unharmed, through the automatic doors and into the bread aisle.

NOVEMBER 2002

life in the asteroid belt

Death. Grief. Illness. Another death. More grieving. Anger. Terror.

I don't know about you, but I think George and I are both showing signs of getting a little burned out from our years up here in the asteroid belt.

Don't get me wrong. I'm not saying it doesn't have its own uniquely dark and startling beauty. And the sudden whoosh of the hurtling asteroids can surely take your breath away.

Of course we were disoriented at first, blasted without warning into space. Still, full of purpose and adrenaline, we were able to bounce around and equilibrate pretty quickly.

But even in the face of our lightning reflexes, our balletic flexibility and acrobatic teamwork, sometimes asteroids just appeared to materialize out of nowhere, knocking one or both of us in the gut or the head.

And now, after years of maintaining this nonstop level of alertness that you can imagine living in an asteroid belt requires, we're tired.

Gravity seems to be working against us. Our timing is off. Those slow-moving missiles we'd easily have ducked in our prime are beaning us even before we turn around.

We're irritable, we're touchy. We're taking offense. We're giving it. Sometimes we even start to think that it's really us hurling those asteroids at each other. On purpose. Ouch. Stop it.

That hurt.

It's distracting. It's hard to think straight. Lord knows, it's hard to communicate. It's time for us to get back down to earth, if we could only figure out the way.

NOVEMBER 2002

time out for romance

I think what I need right now is a love story. And what luck. I've got my all-time favorite right here.

Imagine a Friday night dance at a junior high gym. September 1960, blond wood floor slippery with wax, everyone in socks, girls fast dancing, boys along the wall, Sam Cooke's sweet voice infusing the air with longing.

There I am, way over there in the corner by the doors, almost twelve, white ankle socks, harlequin glasses, wide-eyed with seventh grade jitters and rock and roll, drinking in the scene with my best friend, Beth.

A slow dance starts. A cute boy walks toward us from the other side of the floor. He asks Beth to dance. I know his name. He's in Beth's homeroom. It's George.

When they're done, he walks her back and turns to me. "Me? Sure, I'll dance!" They're playing Put Your Head on my Shoulder.

My palms are icy. "Cold hands, warm heart," he says.

We're moving now, but we're each bouncing to the rhythm of a different part of the beat. We can't get it right. We laugh. The song ends. He walks me back to Beth.

And that's that. I'm hooked for life, not that I realize it that night. But it's true.

By the next time we dance together, we've each had a too-young marriage, one daughter apiece, a divorce and twenty-five years in which we've seen each other only once—except in dreams, of course.

This time love hits me over the head like a sledge hammer. No way out. Sometimes just looking at him takes my breath away, I'm not making this up. In the middle of one night I drive over to his house in my nightgown.

What the hell, I'm crazy about him. And can you believe it? He loves me, too.

We dance together until we're drenched with sweat. We get married.

You can see why I like this story so much. Anyway, the first few years together are pretty simple and sweet. George says stuff like, "Can a person be too happy?" And I don't have to tell you, that kind of thing can't go on forever.

But don't worry, this doesn't have a sad ending, or any ending at all. I'm just saying euphoria has its limits. You get hungry, you have to do the dishes, get back to work, mop up the flood in the basement, call 911 when your mother-in-law has a heart attack, take care of your grandchildren when your son-in-law gets cancer. It can't all be simple or sweet, life.

But this morning, I have a long dream that I'm married to George, but somehow not, you know how it can be in dreams. Because somehow at the same time I'm still married to my first husband, and he's holding me captive in the house. He has some kind of monitors, and he can see who I'm calling on the phone. A couple of times I'm able to sneak a few brief calls to George, but I can't see him, and I feel so alone.

Of course in reality he's right here next to me the whole time, breathing slow and steady on his jumbled pillows in the gray morning light. And when I wake up from my dream, I reach over and grab hold of his arm, heavy and warm from the covers, and I put my head, like the old song said, on his shoulder.

FEBRUARY 2003

a month before war

At least

when the radio wakes us this morning they don't say that war has already started.

At least

the video on the 11 o'clock news last night showing empty shelves at the grocery stores was about the forecast for snow.

At least

we haven't worried for a while about anthrax when we open the mail.

At least

the Pope is in favor of peace.

Every night

we hear the fighter planes flying over our house and Bush's voice on the radio threatening, promising war. And a couple of weeks ago they were telling us to buy water and batteries and to pick a room to tape ourselves inside of.

But at least

here's another snowy morning to let the dog out in the yard, to think about what the kids are doing at school, to read the paper together at the kitchen table, and, when our gazes rise to the window, to see all three violets on the sill blooming at one time—pale pink, white, and deep purple blossoms with centers the yellow of a crayon-colored sun.

FEBRUARY 2006

praise for our rubbermaid mailbox

Three years ago last September

George and I went to Alaska, our first vacation in a long time, and when we got home, Jenny and the kids surprised us with a new green Rubbermaid mailbox from Home Depot to replace the old light blue plastic one that had been whacked with a baseball bat by someone in a passing car more than once.

"Thank you!" we say, though later George says to me, "Why'd she do that? We don't need a new mailbox. The old one is perfectly good."

So the new one stays in its carton in the garage for a long time.

A couple of years later

George and I have a Saturday when we both feel like tackling the mess in the garage, clearing out rusty toy trucks and sodden papers and dismembered boxes, and by the time we come across the carton with the Rubbermaid mailbox, we're in the spirit of renewal.

So George brings it out, along with a couple of two-by-fours from his wood collection on the back shelf and puts it up at the end of the driveway.

We take to it right away, round and sleek, sturdy and green, doors in both front and back. Sometimes, driving in the country, we pass a house along the highway with a mailbox just like ours, and we say, "Look! They've got a Rubbermaid mailbox just like ours!"

I know. It sounds pretty ridiculous. But you know how it is when you've been driving for hours, and you're both feeling the hum of the open road—the littlest thing can be a delight. Like, if you pass a car just like yours, you say, "Look! It's our twin!" Don't you?

Well, anyway, there must be something irresistible about bashing mailboxes with bats, because it keeps on happening to ours. But with the Rubbermaid mailbox, no visible injury at all, just a tilt from vertical to diagonal, which George can easily remedy each time.

And then, sometime over this past winter

when we go out one morning to get the paper, we notice a big jagged hole in the back door of our mailbox. Someone must have exploded a firecracker or a little bomb in there during the night. But aside from the damage to the back door, the mailbox holds firm.

And just a few weeks ago

backing out of our curving driveway in the dark after getting home from a family trip to a bar mitzvah in Cleveland, my dad turns a little hard to the left and gets stuck in the mud in front of our mailbox.

From the porch we can hear his rear wheels spinning, no traction to move forward, and as George runs down the driveway, arms waving, yelling, "Stop! Stop!" Dad revs the engine and hits the mailbox dead on.

It sounds like a gunshot when the two-by-fours snap. I know how bad he must feel. It was only last month when I backed into a parked car across the street from us. Really shakes your confidence.

But not our mailbox. George digs a new hole for it on the other side of the driveway the next day and pounds it in with some posts from his wood collection. And to look at it, except for that hole in its back door, you'd never have guessed it wasn't brand new.

And then for a week afterwards

when Kevin and I go out to get the mail, along with bills and junk flyers and catalogs from L.L. Bean, there are pine needles and twigs and curling brown leaves inside.

"The wind must be blowing them in through that hole in the back door," I say, looking around at the breezeless blue sky.

It doesn't make sense until George figures out that it has to be birds building a nest, starting from scratch after we've swept out the fruits of their hard labors every time we pick up our mail.

It's easy to see why they persisted, such a snug shelter. So superior to the hazards of the traditional branch.

But

this is our mailbox, not a birdhouse. And even though George is well known for his soft spot when it comes to birds, I think you'll understand why he unhinges the little back door and brings it into the kitchen and tapes up the hole with duct tape, taking care, of course, not to leave any sticky sides exposed that the birds might get stuck to when they come back to check on their ideal nest, which, sad to say, has turned out to be too good to be true.

Not like the mailbox itself, which has exceeded all expectations.

letting go

JANUARY 2002

reunion

I saw him yesterday, for the first time in almost nine years.

He's heavier now and red-faced. He doesn't seem to be wearing his teeth anymore. His neck is thick, his cheeks sag, his mouth is sunken. And the expression on his broad face is as dark as ever.

Strangely, his voice has changed into a version of his father's voice, minus his father's hearty tone. After all those years dominated by his voice, I wouldn't recognize it now.

His elderly cousin, Phyllis, says to me, "I think he would have been all right if he hadn't fried his brain. You just have to talk to him for five minutes to know he's not all there."

My tormentor.

The thing, finally, about having been a battered wife, is that you can never escape the shame, the implication of complicity, the "she must have liked it… she must have needed it somehow," like the rape victim who wore a skimpy dress into a dark alley.

I haven't lived with him for almost thirteen years, after being married to him for more than twenty. I saw him a few times in court while I was divorcing him and once more at our daughter's wedding and not again until yesterday, at his father's funeral.

I've made a mistake, I keep thinking, driving to the cemetery through the cold rain with our daughter Jenny and grandson Kevin, who's reading a book in the back seat. "A hundred and sixty-three pages," he says.

I shouldn't be here.

Jenny says, "You shouldn't let him scare you away."

The night before, in bed, George said, "I don't understand. Why are you going if it makes you feel so bad?"

I tell him, I don't want to stay away out of fear.

So I choose my clothes and get my hair blow-dried straight and remember to drink plenty of water.

We find our way to the cemetery on time. Walking into the military chapel, all three of us try to squeeze under one umbrella, and we get the giggles. But not for long, not after we pass the sentries lined up out front in the rain and through the doors.

Then I see him for the first time in almost nine years.

When we were married, there were hardly any days, after the first few years, when he didn't spend some hours yelling at me.

Sometimes first thing in the morning, sometimes in the middle of the night, tearing the covers off me and making me stand and listen to him until he was satisfied with the authenticity of my contrition for whatever had made him mad.

(And how do you make someone stand by the bed for hours in the middle of the night? It's not mysterious. You make them believe that you'll hurt them if they don't. And you make them believe they'd deserve it.)

You'd never put up with that?

Lucky you.

After the funeral, I pick George up from work, and we drive forty-five minutes through the rain to the wake, at my ex-sister-in-law's house. George and I are kidding around a little as we walk down the driveway. Three smokers are standing in the darkness outside the front door. I recognize two of them and smile hello and smile at the third, just another face in the dark.

And it's him.

I hear George, a couple of steps behind me, greet him, as I step inside.

I can see him out of the corner of my eye, while I talk to people I'm glad to see, to stand in front of—uncoupled from him.

At one point, his sister asks me if I know where Jenny is. When I find her, she's standing in the darkened entryway, talking with him. I don't want to be the one to interrupt, and I start to walk around them.

"Suse," I hear him say.

Yes?

"I brought this for you," he says, handing me a set of wood and cork coasters.

"Coasters," I say. "Thanks."

"Don't you remember them?" he asks.

"No. I don't."

"They were your grandparents'," he says, advancing toward me, his narrow eyes on mine.

"I don't remember them. But thank you."

And I walk away.

How not-nice of me, right? A conciliatory gesture on his part, and if it was kind of pathetic—the wooden coaster stand held together with a red rubber band—didn't that make it more important to respond kindly? Not numbly. Not turning my back on him.

Maybe Eleanor Roosevelt would've been kind to him. Maybe you would. As for me, I can't bear to talk to him. I feel menace and accusation and manipulation, and I turn away.

Is this the way it will always be? Is this as far as I'm going to get? Will I be trying to escape from him, yelling at him, "I don't love you anymore," in my dreams for the rest of my life? Will I always be afraid of him?

Even standing in his sister's living room, smiling, being smiled at, George there with me, I feel that just those things—just our smiling presence—might rouse the beast to avenge our intrusion.

And behind that fear, huddling in a dark corner in the back of the cave, is that old feeling that I've brought it on myself. That I shouldn't have come. That I was wrong to presume. That our presence is an insult to him, an invasion of his space.

That, at the very least, for God's sake, if I'm going to be there, I should be nice to him.

Is that true?

Or is it just more of the tired old same?

Am I ever going to get past this point? Earlier today I thought about those mediation programs in prisons, where victims are brought together with the criminals who did them harm. Because—wasn't I the victim?

Yes—responsibility, self-determination, choice, I know. I agree. It's the way I've always told this story. Who wants to be a victim?

Yelled at, threatened, mortified, frightened, lied to, intimidated, shoved, bruised, knocked down, deprived of sleep. Checkbook confiscated, car keys taken, birthday presents thrown in the trash. No offense too obscure to rage about: vitamins I forgot to take, crumbs left on the table, onions not sliced small enough. I complained, I cried, I apologized, I denied the obvious. I stayed. Long.

I'm the victim. This is progress?

I don't like the way it sounds. Poor me, like that. But what if I'd been robbed? Is it shameful to say you're a victim of robbery? Even if maybe you could have done something to avoid it—not stopped at the ATM after dark, moved to a better part of town, whatever—the robber is still the one who gets arrested. Not you.

So George says, "What would you ask him if you met with him? Would you want to find out why he did those things to you?"

What? No. I wouldn't ask him anything.

I wouldn't want him to say anything at all, for once. He's the one, after all, don't forget, who never yielded the floor, who never shut up, the one who yelled for hours. Yes, hours. I want to be the one to talk this time.

Don't interrupt me.

But what would it help to say?

You hurt me. You were mean to me. You lied to me. You scared me. You took advantage of my insecurity and my conscience. You humiliated me in front of everybody. You stole my money. You were drunk and raging and broke things and screamed at me in the night. You threatened to leave me by the side of the road. You told me I was ugly. You told me I was dumb.

I don't care if you're screwed up. I don't care what your mother did to you when you were young or how long your father was away from home.

Stop taking it out on me.

You were wrong to take it out on me.

You hurt me. It still hurts.

And coasters? If they belonged to my grandparents, what were you doing with them anyway? So you're giving back something you took from me?

Big deal. That's nothing. You took twenty years from me. You took my trust and my affection and my youthful hopes and my multitudinous apologies and my countless turns of the other cheek and my forgiveness and my trying again, again.

Thief. You stole all my feeling for you, all my sympathy, threw them all away, drove them into a ditch. And I still feel damaged, still bruised. I'm still scared. I'm still mad.

I'm so tired of it.

I wish you knew what you did. I wish you would tell everyone how wrong you were, how sorry you are.

I wish that I could look at you and feel, "Okay, I'm myself, you're you, whatever it is that you are. You're not a part of me, anymore."

And I wish you would sprout white flapping wings and fly away from my heart and rain down good-bye blessings as you disappear at last into the cloudy gray sky.

OCTOBER 2002

letting go 101

Wow.

This is a big class. Don't worry if you can't find a seat, we won't be using the chairs much anyway.

Oh, and there won't be any written syllabus. You'll just be expected to memorize everything you learn and then successfully incorporate it into your daily life.

What was that—the hand in the back of the room? Oh, right. We get that question every year. Yes, we know it's not fair. And you're right, almost all of you will fail. But this is a required course. You can always take it again.

In fact, you'll have to.

First off

I'd like to see everyone who's here because you still want to be skinny or look the same as you did when you were 25, and everyone who thinks they should be able to make their hair look like someone's on TV.

I want all of you into the pool with the eight-year-olds. Everyone holding onto the sides, no pushing, I know there are a lot of you, but there's plenty of room. Okay.

Now everyone let go of the side with your hands and shove off hard with both your feet. That's it.

Let go!

Now.

Over here I need everyone who makes to-do lists, all of you who outlined your class notes, you people who order the same thing every time you go out to a restaurant, those of you who filter your drinking water—

you know who you are—and everyone who goes back into the house to make sure you've turned off the stove.

All of you into this boat. That's it. Now, everyone grab an oar, and let's row out into the middle of the ocean. All right. Good.

Now, everybody out of the boat. Don't worry, you can hold onto the sides when you're in the water. Good. Good.

Now. Everyone let go! I know I said you could hold on. But you can't. I'm rowing away! Now let go!

Let go!

Okay.

Now may I please see everyone who still dreams that you could have been a contender, those of you who yearn to be appreciated and understood, all of you who still believe that goodness and fairness are rewarded in this life, and everybody who's angry.

I need you to form a line, no shoving, angry people. It doesn't matter who's first. That's it. Now everybody climb this cliff and wait for me when you get to the top.

Good job. I'll bet some of you surprised yourselves with your own strength. Now, all of you, move over here right to the edge. It's all right, hold onto the railing if it helps.

Now jump! Come on. Keep it moving. You can't jump if you're holding on. Let go of the railing!

Let go!

Who's left?

All right. Let me see all you mothers and grandmothers. And I want to see all the parents who hope to teach your children everything you've learned from life. And all you interveners here who still trust in words to convince, to heal, to change, to save. And everyone who's still trying to keep the people you love safe from harm.

Over here right now. Yes, I know it's getting dark, but I want you to walk into the middle of that moonless forest up ahead. That's it, keep walking, don't worry about landmarks. It's too dark to see them anyway. Okay. Everybody grab onto the nearest tree.

Now, let go. No, there aren't any maps. We ran out years ago. You'll just have to figure out how to find the way on your own. Now, let go!

Let it go!

Well, that was a pretty good start.

But I see that most of you still seem to be having a lot of trouble letting go on very basic levels. You mothers and you angry people, especially— I'd highly recommend you check out the list of tutors on the bulletin board in the hall.

As for the rest of you, we'll be working on exercises based on related questions, such as what's left to hold on to, how to hold on while letting go, and who you are after you let go of the things you thought you needed most.

See you next week!

MARCH 2003

violets

When John died, someone sent us a big basket of violets, purple, pink, magenta, white, all at the height of flowering. There were flowers all over the house at the time, hard to find places to put them all, once they walked in the door.

My sister-in-law, Janie, sent an orchid with translucent white petals and rubbery, curving green leaves. So elegant, so graceful, I made a place for it in the kitchen window right away, between Kevin's popsicle stick picture frame; the glass vial with Melanie's miniature shell collection; the flower-printed paper cup with my sister Mimi's peace candle from New Year's Eve; the white plastic Abe Lincoln, lone survivor of my brother David's Civil War soldiers set; the lotion jar; the broken snow globe from Alaska; the plastic tiger with only three legs intact since an unfortunate incident with one of the dogs, still good otherwise; and whatever other plants were already there. I don't remember which they were anymore.

The violets in their basket get shuffled from room to room. When their fuzzy leaves droop, I pour in some water, just enough care to let them not die. My brain clouds over when I look too closely at the way they've been bunched together in their clear plastic tubs.

After a while

the basket seems to take up too much space, so I poke holes in the bottoms of the tubs with a paring knife and set them on dishes. A year or so passes. The violets hang on with minimal help from me. But no more flowers.

I'm a putterer, a straightener. I move piles from table to shelf. I commune with my rooms and imagine ways to rearrange, to harmonize, to fine-tune.

Mostly this takes place slowly, when the other people who live here are somewhere else or watching TV or on the phone, and they rarely seem to realize that anything has changed.

If I ask, "Did you notice the coffee table?" George or Jenny might say, "Nice."

Or they might say, "Is it different?"

In this way, weeks pass, and seasons, the programmable watch that John bought to try to keep track of his medication schedule, just before he got too sick to use it, beeping in muffled staccato from its hiding place somewhere in the house every night at twelve.

And one day while I'm sloshing water into a bunch of the violets, I have a moment of clarity. I can buy pots. I can gently disentangle their roots. I can transplant them.

The kids and I cover the kitchen table with newspaper, slit open a bag of soil and pour it into the new pots. Leaning on their elbows, the kids watch as I carefully cut perimeters around each violet through the dirt in the plastic tubs, and we take turns tapping the bottoms with the handle of a butter knife to loosen their roots from the old soil.

The dirt feels crumbly and soft on our fingers as we pat it in and around the newly potted plants. There's just enough room for three of them in the kitchen window.

More time passes.

September 11. Terror alerts. Relentless headlines for war. Marches for peace. Jenny and the kids move to their own place, not far away, but I miss them so much when they first go that I walk around our house and cry, while I straighten and sort through drawers and rearrange bookcases and haul the old, stained playroom rug out to the garage.

There are a lot fewer dishes to do, of course. But even with just two people, you spend some time every day or so standing at the sink, looking out at the yard, your eyes lingering on the plants in the window sill, Janie's orchid and John's three violets.

(The orchid, I have to take a minute to say, that plant must be some kind of orchid genius, its milky petals blooming for six months at a stretch, replaced by new ones just as the old ones fade, shiny leaves curving left and right, silvery roots slithering out of the pot and onto the window sill.)

But the violets. I want them to bloom again. I want flowers.

So I water them and turn them, and I paint blue squiggly lines on one of the pots to give it a jauntier look.

Months go by.

And then the one with large, rounded leaves blooms white, square-petaled flowers. And a month or two later, the one with profusions of small, heart-shaped leaves blooms pink, primrose-petaled flowers. And a month or so after that, the last one, the violet with long, pointy, dark-green leaves blooms purple-violet, frilly-petaled, white-edged flowers with tiny balls of yellow in the center of each one—all three violets blooming at one time, together in the window. And the orchid, of course, arching whitely and greenly behind them.

And I say, "George, look at this purple one!" I want to invite my mother over to see them. I want the neighbors to come and take a look. I want to paint them large on acid-free paper. I want to memorize them.

So here we are. It's now.

George finds John's programmable watch underneath some things on the bathroom shelf and puts it on. The kids come and spend the night. I putter. I do the dishes.

The President is on TV, prime time press conference, a big deal. I can't watch. But I read in the paper this morning that he says twelve more days and that's it, we go to war. Nothing can stop him. The bombs are ready. Twelve more days.

Boom.

And I sign petitions and go to meetings and marches and speak earnestly with friends. And I stand in my kitchen.

And I water my violets.

POSTSCRIPT, APRIL 2011

one day the bird flies away

The cage is open, the window, too.
A rare occurrence.

How is it
that the bird
knows?
Do its
feathers feel
the fullness
in the flow
of air?
Does chance carry it to the sill?

Does it know in its bones,
the way birds know how to
swoop and turn with the flock,
who to follow,
where to lead,
when to fly?

The bird finds the sky in the blink of an eye. George runs outside, scanning the branches, calling its name. But it's already gone. Poof.

George is sad. "Keep the bird,"
I told him years ago, not
that I really wanted him to.
But he wouldn't budge,
and I was sick of arguing.
So he took me at my word
and kept the bird. And I wrote

a story about it and called it "The Year of the Bird" to try to make sense
of everything that was happening. Including that.

Once in a while, someone asks, "Do you still have that bird?"
But when it's just us alone, on that subject at least, there's quiet.

Winter was long this year. The first day of spring came
and went. But the cold has kept the daffodils blooming.
And now the birds are flocking back.

There's a cardinal whistling
in the front yard.
My friend, Kathy, saw a bluebird
in the woods last weekend.
And at the shopping mall,
geese are nesting outside the
entrance to J. C. Penney's.
There's a sign taped to the
glass door warning
customers
to step
with
care.

Here in the living room, the dog is restless,
anxious for a walk. George is stalling her
with a toy. "Just one more minute,"
I tell him. "I'm almost finished writing."
But I can't find my way to the end.
Endings are hard. Let it go.
For now, the dog needs a walk.
Maybe the words will come later.

thanks

These stories are suffused with loving memories of our son-in-law, John Lyons, who graced our lives with his kindness, courage, good sense and gentle ways; my mother-in-law, Jean Spangler, whose spunk, forthrightness and love of living never faltered, and who could make any of life's lemons into lemonade; and my sister-in-law, Susan E. Spangler, whose keen eye never missed a stitch, who honored me with her friendship, and who knew how to say just about anything in a way that would make you laugh. I'm deeply grateful to my mother, Barbara Scheiber, for her inspired observations and her ever-ready editing.
To my father, Walt Scheiber, my brothers, David Scheiber and Robert Scheiber, and my sister-in-law, Janie Scheiber, for their unfailing encouragement.
To Peter Carlson, Kate Horsley, Lou Cunningham and my sister, Miriam Seidel, for their invaluable suggestions. And to Minnie Wiens, Steve Malone, Kathe Barnier, Kathy Oehl, Pat Einhorn, Emily Dean, Brigid Monaghan, Ian Davie and Vanessa Davie for living these stories with us, for reading them, and for sharing so many others, most of them never written down. To our daughters—Jenny, for her strength, her resourcefulness, and her love; and Gretchen, for always carrying us in her heart. To our grandchildren, Kevin, Melanie, Jeremy—and Matthew, who was born after these stories were written—for each of their unique, bright, and beautiful selves. And of course, to my husband, George, for his strong arms and his good heart, for hanging in and holding on for better and for worse, and for setting off with me each new year into who-knows-what's-next.

Susan Spangler is an award-winning graphic designer, illustrator, painter, writer and homeschool teacher. She and her husband, George, share their home with two young dogs, an elderly cat and fluctuating numbers of fish and kids. To see more of her pictures and words, go to www.susanspangler.com and http://theunschool-ablekid.com.

www.ingramcontent.com/pod-product-compliance
Lightning Source LLC
Chambersburg PA
CBHW041158290426
44109CB00002B/57